Still Life with Towel and Sand

Still Life with Towel and Sand

Poems by

Eileen Moeller

© 2024 Eileen Moeller. All rights reserved.
This material may not be reproduced in any form, published,
reprinted, recorded, performed, broadcast,
rewritten, or redistributed without
the explicit permission of Eileen Moeller.
All such actions are strictly prohibited by law.

Cover design by Shay Culligan
Cover art by Susan Barnes
The original painting (before crop) was 19.75" x 47.25".
Title: Beach Lineup
Medium: Oil/Canvas
C. 2007 Sold in 2007 to private collector
Website: www.susanbarnesfineart.com

ISBN: 978-1-63980-553-2

Kelsay Books
502 South 1040 East, A-119
American Fork, Utah 84003
Kelsaybooks.com

To Sylvan June Morning Moeller: This Little Family

Acknowledgments

Much gratitude goes to Kelsay Books for their support in making this book a reality, and to artist Susan Barnes, for her beautiful cover art.

Earlier versions of some of the poems appeared in the following publications, for which I am grateful:

Cries of the Spirit: A Celebration of Women's Spirituality (Beacon Press, 1987): "domestic poem"
Finding What You Didn't Lose (John Fox, 1995): "domestic poem"
Writing Women (London, 1997): "The Year of the Plum-Colored Bathing Suit"
Ars Medica (Canada, 2012): "The Black Dog"
We'Moon Desk Calendar (2024): "Duck Harbor"

Finally, I want to thank poet, Michael Gervasio, for planting the seeds of this book in me, by sharing a group of his poems about a family vacation, in workshop. Michael left us too many years ago, and is sorely missed.

Contents

What Salty Tide Is This?

Salt Dolls	15
Each Summer	16
Newcomb Hollow Beach	17
At Gull Pond	18
The Swimmer	19
Butterfly Quiet	20
Cucumber Salad	21
Wellfleet Harbor	22
Salt Marsh	23
At Pied Piper	24
Domestic Poem	25
Tell Me About the Blue Box of Your Childhood	26
It All Begins in Water	27
Long Pond	28
Portuguese Bakery	29
Lieutenant Island	30
My Heart Is a Red Minivan	31
Baby on the Beach	32
The Year of the Plum-Colored Bathing Suit	33
Sea Urchin Beach	34
Sleeping Boy	35
Cinnamon	36
Adrift on the Silence	37
A Day Can Decompose	38
Post Mortem	39
I've Been Dreaming About Houses	40
I Remember Spending Whole Days	41
Girls	42
Mooncussers	44
Cohoon Hollow Beach	45
Amphibiology	47

Race Point Beach	48
Fresh Air Child	49
A Mermaid Girl	50
Conversation with My Mother	51
Those Blackberry Years	53
Round Pond	55
The Black Dog	56
Sloan-Kettering	58
Window	59
Corn Hill at Low Tide	61
Reach for Me	62
Ode to the Moon Snail	63
Duck Harbor	64
Mother of Pearl	65
Atwood Higgins House	66
Beehive Oven	67
The Body's Errand	68
Masher	69
When Fog Is Afoot	70
Wellfleet Pier	71
Whale Watch	72
Another Word for Mother Is Water	74
Special	75
Kite	76

What Salty Tide Is This?

Salt Dolls

Every year we make a pilgrimage
to this gray-green mother,
laying ourselves out,
like pink infant mice,
on the beach at her salty feet,
as sky curves its protective blue
over us, and the pearl moon
pulls the tides with silken threads.

She spills away, then slides back,
writing her name in tide pools around us,
then erasing it in a crash of white.
Her pull and push, like the birth our cells remember.

And we wade in—
to learn what we're made of,
to dissolve into the glistening
core of what's beautiful,
wave upon wave.

Each Summer

We inhabit a different house,
become seasonal ghosts on short term
hauntings, neutrinos flying everywhere,
skin cells and sleep breath, cooking smells,
lost hair, silliness and morning chatter,
afternoon bickering and good night kisses,
the scents of our cleaning products and toiletries.

Each house needs airing out, each needs ritual
cleansing, small exorcisms carried out
by linens and pillows brought from home,
by incense and music, always a little music.

For a week or two, we try them on
like someone else's shoes that don't quite fit.

One with a deck, overlooking the marsh,
has terrible furniture, the bliss of one's outdoor shower
is offset by hard beds, or windows that won't open.
The kitchens have too little counter space, they're missing
a corkscrew, pot lids, serving bowls big enough for a family.

We try to leave them as lightly as we found them,
these summer affairs, we're thankful for,
but will probably never see again. Best to
slink off quickly, sad but full of longing,
to get back home to the one we love.

Newcomb Hollow Beach

Pants legs rolled
they stand holding hands,
washed by the wing of the outgoing tide:
the liquid glass that platters beneath their feet,
then suddenly pulls so hard the other way
they look rooted, where they stand,
to this curving edge of the world.

How playful and openhearted,
how heedless of the water's
burning cold. How bold
to enter such enormous mystery.

My husband and our two babies
chasing, and being chased by the sea,
tidal creatures I watch from
my world of white paper and words.

At Gull Pond

Pink water bird
goes swimming,
all gangly legged and glory,
her hair: a waterfall of golden streaks
as she stands and shakes,
all dynamism and zing.

Which pulls a sigh
from her tired father,
and pushes at the silence
wrapped around her mother,
who is presently lost
in the pages of a book.

Both of them
so far beyond her reach,
a still life with towels
and sand on a narrow beach.

The Swimmer

Slides through my days in measured strokes,
at one with his element, no purposeless action,
no energy wasted. The swimmer is
my economy, his grief spending slowly.
I watch him, imitating
the long liquid breaths myself.

The swimmer glides through me
silent and silver. He lets the water lift him
across the liquid sky above.
I am filled with love watching him,
his elbows like slow motion wings,
the sun limning his wake.

I flick my tail in deep water,
wishing I too could rise
out of this cloud of darkness.

Butterfly Quiet

Fish too small to see
nibbling at your knee,
the snap of a single hair
breaking, tickle of eyelash,
fine dry sand spilling through
your fingers, your hand cupping
your ear, the smallest blueberry
falling, a dewdrop burning off
in the morning, a dot, a dash,
cat's fur rubbing against the
sofa, feathers afloat
after preening,
a cumulus cloud wisping to
invisibility, the Ferris wheel
on the boardwalk when you're
so far away it fits on the tip of
your finger, a teenage girl's
sigh behind glass, dust
motes hopping around
you, as you follow
that piece of color
and light, through
the garden, with
your eyes.

Cucumber Salad

The final draft of our dinner,
a last revision before
it goes to press:

the long slender vegetable,
moist and cool in my hand,
giving itself, not without resistance,
to the blade of the slicer,
its pale rounds a moon
alphabet against the muddy
plain of the cutting board,

onion in thinnest rings,
repeating a whisper
on still nights
that bite with heat,
gauzy alfalfa sprouts
like green tipped sperm,
fertile as new dug earth.

One must bathe them then,
in polarities of flavor,
sweet and sour completions
to send collisions across our tongues.

We'll see things anew,
as images wilt in the dark bowl,
a lily pond midsummer
beckoning, beckoning to us,
languid, all moss and dragonflies.

Yes, I say, glad to be transported.
The clink of forks and knives for punctuation.

Wellfleet Harbor

His fish is belly white
and shark-like,
but he holds it up,
because all he sees
are its silver stripes,
and how big it is,
that he caught it by himself,
and the way it flails
as he waves it back and forth.

He shows it to everyone
who looks his way.
He's a lighthouse, beaming.

Here, his father says,
Hurry up. Put it in the cooler.
That's right, his mother hisses.
That's enough!
We've all had enough!

Salt Marsh

Small as beetles
in the dry grass:
tiny toads
are everywhere,
evading little hands.

A sweet-eyed girl
begs her father for the net
and he says no,
yanking it away from her.

At first, she cries,
burning with lost possibility.

Then she turns away,
and leaning over,
cups one in her hands.

At Pied Piper

You watch a little man playing out his malice,
and reeling it back in, like a prize catch:
sitting and smoking across from his
doppelganger of a boy, who squirms to get
away from his gaze, and in doing so,
knocks his fork to the floor, which gives him
a chance to climb down and pick it up.

Of course, the man is on him lightning quick,
like an iron fist, or jaws on a piece of bait.
Eat with yer fingers now, he growls. *Serves ya right!*

Later, you hear him bragging to the waitress.
Yeah, he nods, emerging from a gray cloud,
that boy is Pa's main man.

Domestic Poem

Nightfall I sink
into dishwash meditation:

steaming china prayer wheels
crystalline bells of a lost horizon

breathing slows, din and
lull of running water from crockery mandalas

moist heat muscles soften
Zen poems drip from silverware

air hums out a chanting
cleansing melody

washing the frantic stew of a day
down the drain along with the suds

those transient rainbow things
thin skin of the passing instant.

Tell Me About the Blue Box of Your Childhood

Tell me where it took you, where away, away from what?
Tell me what it rescued, how it opened into eternity,
how you remember climbing inside, its blue walls
folding neatly around you, the way the box
clicked shut, and all the voices disappeared.

Tell me what kind of fears you contained this way.
Tell me where you hide your collection of blue box days,
keep them squirreled away, so you can take them out
and try to live them again. Were you tight as a pin-curl
when the blue box found you? Were you whirling in
place like an imprisoned Dervish? Were you a human
cannonball aimed at your parents every morning,
as they smoked themselves awake? Did they take to
overfeeding you, to quell you into silence?
Who were you before that blue box sat on the shelf?

Tell me why you closed it when you did.
Tell me what it sings when you open the lid.

It All Begins in Water

I remember splashing
in the warm soup of Crestwood Lake,
and my father arching himself away
from my small reaching arms
as I sunk into brown murk
streaked with pale shoots of sun

as I paddled frantically toward him,
instinct holding my breath for me,
the water alive with dust,
and when he caught me,
and lifted me up,
I gasped like an old trout,
and it made him laugh:
a realer laugh than any
I can remember after that.

I'll never forget those lessons,
or get over that my father
couldn't learn them himself:
the reaching, the will,
the struggle to rise to the light.

When he died, I tried to picture him
drifting slowly down river,
borne by powerful currents
out to the ocean, wrapped
in a schooling halo of sunnies.

And the little fish inside me
stretched toward the sound of my voice
as if I were crooning a lullaby
calling Daddy, Daddy, like that
over and over across the dark.

Long Pond

Another word for child is
tadpole about to grow legs.
You can see them emerging,
as you squint through
light that's become too bright.

You suddenly want to dive
beneath the water's cool surface,
hear nothing, watch the tiny
sand-colored fish dart and stop,
be simple-minded, watch them wriggle
and play, lift them up and throw them
into the water, churning things up,
dizzy with mischief and hilarity.

But they'll have none of it.

There are books to be read,
sunglasses to put on, beach
chairs to tilt toward the sun.

Portuguese Bakery

They're at the last table
eating their lunch in silence,
Him: round as a beetle,
Her: fine-waisted, small as an ant.

His shirt reads NYPD,
but she treats him like her baby:
before he's finished
she's up and scurrying off
for a huge wedge of cake
and two forks.

What is it?
He wants to know.
Rum, she murmurs,
pausing to heighten the drama.
Rum with Boston Crème.

Soon their forks
dance like antennae,
and I catch them
glancing sideways
to where we sit with our kids:
a noisy chorus of crickets.

Lieutenant Island

The green flies hurl themselves
hard against the windows we just rolled up
to keep them from tearing chunks of our flesh away.
Flesh and blood, new blood, blood intoxication
is what they need to take them far away
from this wild lonely place,
exposed every day as they are
to a scouring wind.

A wind that doesn't want them here,
where houses flounder like beached whales,
and the tide rises over the road,
so the only way in or out
is a one-lane bridge that barely spans
the surge of water, in from the bay,

The green flies wait
for what they crave,
and we sit locked up, tight
as a cluster of empty rentals.

My Heart Is a Red Minivan

Speeding among the dunes,
a glass of claret on wheels
hurtling toward you
after being poured.

Who cares if we're about to crash and burn?

Go on and take a sip, it thumps.
Blood is thicker than both of us.
I'll take my lumps
and you should too.
At least we'll know we're real.

Baby on the Beach

Sit like a little tent and look at your hands
as they fly fat as sparrows in front of your face.

So much space to wave those tiny arms around in,
as your brother's fleet of folded paper boats goes sailing by.

Tongue the breeze while the green flies dip and sway.
Then pat the sand and rub it in your eye.

Cry at the giant birds as they land and gawk,
and to Mama all laid out with her nose in a book.

The light's too bright and hot on your silky skin, isn't it?
Curl your arms and legs to your belly and give her a wail.

When she spreads a blanket out for you in the shade
Spin yourself around belly down. Show her happiness.

Go ahead: nod and coo and creep, until your
head drops down all at once and into sleep.

The Year of the Plum-Colored Bathing Suit

my breasts were blue-veined porcelain
and full of milk for the baby.
I waited for you to notice
them spilling, a soft waterfall,
wished you'd ask me to put
marmalade on them at tea.

All summer I offered you sweet rolls,
hoping you'd cup them lightly
in soft but insistent fingers.

Instead, all you could see
was what had to be done, you
changed and rocked the baby
while I read my book,
and rolled around
in the shallows, playing
with the older one for hours.

Sea Urchin Beach

It looked like the last beach on earth,
Do you remember?
Or maybe the first, primordial,
wind-battered boomerang of land
rushing out to a narrow spit,
crowded with gray speckled
granite eggs that fit just so
in the hollow of your hand,
little bodies pulling hard at our heat.

And scattered among them—
thousands of sea urchin husks,
their tentacles gone, skins
hollow and calcified,
each one inscribed with
a primal braille, beautiful and
other-worldly as Maine's nights,
full of so many stars, in patterns
we sensed, but couldn't decipher.

We were on our honeymoon then,
remember? Fresh from a balsam
forest bath, every one of our cells
intoxicated, and flexible enough
to bend the way saplings do,
to harvest those pale husks,
curving, like the horizon,
toward our future.

Our green hearts were wide open.
We gathered as many as we could.
Remember how we cradled
their delicate heads, as if we'd
birthed them? So filled were we
with the thunder of the tides.

Sleeping Boy

He dreams the world simple
and golden as his hair,

a world that fits in a little hand,
where father can build castles
and mother sleeps
pink cheeked as he is,
and solid as the sand dunes.

He dreams a world that whispers
reassurances, in spite of breakers
and the undertow,
boys like him, running
head-on into the waves,
to be lifted into the air,
as if they were leggy birds,
on the froth, flying so high
they trace the arc joy makes
inside our chests,
and reawaken it
in us as we watch.

Oh yes, he has watchers too.
He's dreaming me to write this down,
and you with your eyes moving over the page,
you bending and holding your chin in your hand
as you turn this coded scrawl back into pictures.

This is how he likes it best:
both of us busy,
adrift on waves of words,
not a question mark
to be had anywhere.

Cinnamon

Seems to come up more often here.
Don't bury the cinnamon,
someone says as you try
to concentrate on the novel you brought.

Who's wearing cinnamon sun block?
We'll look like a handful of red hots
if we don't put up the umbrellas.
What cinnamon lurks in the hearts of men?

A little boy shouts at his father
through a blue Styrofoam noodle,
and all the words are *cinnamon.*
How much cinnamon will it take to
get a man up off a blanket long enough
to play like a boy in the water?

A woman with cinnamon skin
stakes out her territory:
marks it with pails and beach chairs,
one of which she finally drops into,
but not before she grabs her copy of *Dune.*

Adrift on the Silence

At times the mirror increases a thing's value, at times denies it.
—Italo Calvino

I step out of the shower
and see myself in the steamy mirror,
a figure softened and obscured by the blending of opposites:
the heat of the water still in me,
the cool air momentarily warmed and shifting.

How beautiful, I murmur to the glass,
the moons of my breasts, my belly, planetary
and glowing against the dusk of my chest and thighs.

I imagine a series of photographs,
my body idealized like this, gauzed
over by a sudden burst of forgiveness.
Then try on different poses:
leaning forward, then back, the legs at angles,
arms out so she looks like an angel.

Impulsively I wipe the place
on the mirror, where my mouth is, clean.
A beach rose, rose hip, purse full of seeds
that will let them go someday when the time is right.
Another swipe for the eyes, but I see, right away,
this toying with clarity is dangerous.
And now it's too late.

The eyes don't trust the mouth; never have.
They've called the shots all my life:
what to eat, how much, what to wear.
Of course, they notice the tiredness, the sagging,
that my body's orbs are less than celestial.
The eyes know fat when they see it.
The shape shifting session's over, they say,
and who were you kidding anyway?

A Day Can Decompose

Faster than a fish head
left on the dock in the sun.

Ask anyone who's been a hapless witness
to a fight, or heard a string of words

reach out like a hand to slap a cheek.
The sky turns white, the air goes still,
and the water suddenly reeks.

The flies begin to lay
their eggs in your eyes.

Post Mortem

One time I fought with a chicken
for almost an hour trying to pry
the little bag with the heart in it loose.
The chicken wouldn't give it up.
Like an icy mouth unwilling to speak,
it held its inner workings away from me,
its tiny frozen worries and wastes
until I had to get the knife out,
humiliate us both by sawing and hacking
the whole thing apart, shredding the paper,
the little bits of redness flying like shrapnel.

I felt so wounded I threw it in the garbage,
and sank deeper into the kitchen chair,
stare fixed on the front of the stove,
while the dishwasher hummed its
relentless, circular journey.

So much is frozen inside me too.
It's always a struggle. What is
stillborn, or won't come into the light,
what remains mysterious, indigestible.

It sat like a lump in my throat, like
the chicken I knew would haunt me.
And here it is, haunting me still.

I've Been Dreaming About Houses

Country houses, with family rooms, in the city,
and pools down in their bellies,
pools dark green as emeralds wearing salmon perfume.

Houses with alphabet microwaves
and labyrinthine hallways
that lead to secret bedrooms,
with big-windowed ballrooms upstairs,
for waltzing along the horizon line,
or bocce with the hubby and kids.

And let's face it, they're in ruins.
They need airing out, remodeling:
ochre-colored ceilings to warm them up.
It's time to get cracking,
stop the raccoons
from nesting in the walls,
to fix and put things right.

It's summer—
and the ocean is pounding out
that old familiar tune.

I Remember Spending Whole Days

at the Jersey shore; coming home,
my skin red, and so hot it gave me chills.
At the end of the dunes a Ferris wheel
sat winking its skeletal clock face, its
lights going on at twilight, calling us,
music blaring, to come and ride.

I remember standing on a jetty once,
watching the ocean breathe in and out.
I was taking LSD, and its symphony
made me feel like a conductor, waving
my wild arms in time to its crashes, slaps,
and sudsy overtures, ravished by
its music, the spray and the wind.

Look, a sailboat is tracing the long
horizon, thin and spectral.
Lit from behind, it looks
like a bag with a candle inside,
the kind that carries
a prayer for the dead.

Each of us is small
as that boat,
don't you think?

Sailing all alone in our heads.
We cut our lives into memory chunks
with time's sharp upturned blade.

Why we feel thin as paper, sometimes,
and carry a torch for the past.

Girls

just come into ripeness,
are in training,
and spilling new breasts
sweet as beach plums.

No sun block for them,
no worries about wrinkles,
just baby oil so their bare bellies shine,
their golden legs throw back the light.

Watch them brush the sand that clings to their calves,
lightly, lightly, their graceful hands.
This one wears a red plaid string bikini.
That one: blue chenille with push-up cups.

Another is in spandex black
which brings out the gold in the hairs
down the small of her back.

All of them walk on tiptoe through the sand,
pelvises tilted down, footing tentative and uneven
as it would be in high heels.

They practice languorous poses, play
paddle ball together, tugging at their tiny bottoms.
Soon they'll receive their assignments:
each one a beloved to manage and please,

men who will stare, and fondle,
their grins speaking worlds.
Girls who will feel defined,
and indefinable all at once.

Later there will be kids to feed on the beach,
to chase and cover with baby sun block,
big umbrellas, T-shirts, and hats.
There will be people to watch and fantasies,
girls on the next towel over,
or gliding along the shore like ravenous birds.

Mooncussers

We toss and turn
while they build their driftwood
fires on the sheets, calling
the makeshift boat, we sail,
to harbor before we've come
round the tip of the Cape.

There's the lighthouse, you say,
and suddenly we're aground
on Nauset beach; surrounded by
demons with knives and clubs.

No, wait a minute. This isn't right.

These aren't our dreams at all.
They're shreds of the past:
shipwrecks that rise to haunt this place
at low tide, beached whales
decomposing along the coastline,
dying outermost houses spilling
their contents into the sea.

Come on. Let's set the past free,
go adrift in a mermaid's purse,
dine on sea pickles
and poor man's pepper
among the dunes.

What say we sing a tune
we've written ourselves.
Call it we never could have
imagined good this good.

Cohoon Hollow Beach

Next to you,
a father paces the sand,
beer in hand,
trying to find a chink
in the metal fence
his family's built around him.

You watch him
correct his kids
as they ignore him.

You turn away
when he badgers the teenage boy,
who cannot seem to sit still,
who moments ago
dove head first into a wave
as it hit the beach,
so, it threw him back on the sand.

You listen as a man clatters his cup
across the bars of a terrible indifference.

And you're a child again, raging
in silence at this alien
who suddenly wants to communicate.

You don't want to speak his language,
punctuated as it is by pop tops
and a bandy-legged strut
that tilts slightly leeward.

Brace yourself, and watch them
stare at their feet as he pitches a fit,
and runs the bucket he told his little girl to empty,

down to the water, dumping out
her whole day's collection of shells
because she wasn't listening
when he told her it's wrong to keep a starfish.

He leaves us all thinking about starfish:
their tenacity, the way they wrap themselves
around their prey, or grow new rays
to replace the ones they've lost.

Amphibiology

Croaker,
you backtrack angel,
your spumey spiel
spools out
stringy as frogspawn across a tarn.

Croaker,
you vapid backbone shadow,
signify will you?

Mizzen mogul,
forego your fourberie
for a change,
and give me something less asomatous.

Croaker,
I want my mind to leap and caper.
I want ideas ponderous and fleshly
as doohickeys
or even dog's soup.

Croaker,
You drizzening fribbler.
Give me at least
a finger full
of fight water.

Race Point Beach

Only after they wash the sand,
off her snow cone, a second time,
do the parents sound a bit cranky,
or finally say *sit down*
to the little girl with both her tiny
hands around a dripping
neon nosegay, its sugary water
lilies undoing themselves—
a reverse Monet—on her bathing suit
and legs in this shifting
un-museum of hot sunny day.

Fresh Air Child

Dark brown and long
as a water bird,
She arches and bends
and dips into the roiling surf
trying to wash off
sand that clings to her skin
like a coverall made of corn meal
she's been made to put on
by the little ones
who buried her
up to her neck
on the beach.

Now pink as a nest
of hairless mice
they sit and stare
at her water dance
itchy to play
new games with this
big talking doll
Mommy brought home
from the train.

But she's flown, at least,
for the rest of the day.
She will not look their way
though they call and call to her
where she sits alone
on the towel her mother
bought her before she left.

A Mermaid Girl

luxuriates in the roiling surf,
a bikini clad girl, who throws her
sausage shaped pre-teen body,
into the waves, while the rest of us
watch her in hooded sweatshirts.

The air is cool but she is singing
to herself, wild and sturdy,
giving in to a loose-limbed reverie,
as the tide dresses her in gowns of green
with foamy white lace.

The bliss on her face is contagious.
I used to cavort at water's edge like this,
remember the splash, the push,
the pull, the slap of the surf,
against my fishtail, being
a piece of flotsam on
the edge of this
teeming world.

Conversation with My Mother

I watch Katie as she runs,
her back to me, toward the waves,
and I see her back, at twelve years old,
is your back, broad shouldered,
curving down to a small high waist,
then the globe of the hips,
smooth and bright in the bathing suit.

I remember how you held her in the hospital.
It was just a month, before she was born,
that we found out you were dying,
and then there she was, like a little pod,
plump with the seeds of another chance.

And my grief for you then,
gone from us before
she was six months old,
was so powerful and long,
she had to take it as all there was of me,
as an ocean that would alternately
rock her and push her under.

Because of that, I think she is
a lover of the moment,
and sturdier than you were,
bound to the world with
a cord she knotted herself,
not looking for a way out,
like you seemed to be,
stronger against the undertow.

I remember you at twelve.
Oh yes, I do, because of all your stories,
so full of romance, in spite of the Depression,

on the brink of something wonderful,
until your father's death pinned you,
like a rogue wave, to the sand,
left you weepy and painfully shy,
still asking, on your fiftieth birthday,
why you had to lose him.

And at first, I asked why too,
over and over. Why did you have to go?
Though it's gotten me nowhere,
but here, I guess,
sitting on the sand watching
as Emmet, who is nine now,
long and lean as Daddy was,
cajoles Katie into building a castle.
My babies, growing up without their grandmother,
while I sit here ruminating on a newfound grief
I know you'd understand:
kids racing headlong into adulthood.

Ma, the waves are curling white
and breaking, the dunes are so
changed in a season by the wind,
How quickly it happens.
Soon these two,
one so much like you,
one so much like Dad,
will sail away from me,
full of their own hungry hope,
and mine, and even what's
left unspent of yours.
How will I ever
be strong enough
to survive it?

Those Blackberry Years

Who knew how precious
and fleeting they were?

All I thought about
was avoiding thorns,
and how to get the best
they had to offer
in late summer heat,
before the birds did,

and teaching our children
to go in early morning,
to gingerly grasp
the ripest black
bubble clusters,
ease them
from the stem,
cradle their juicy
honeycombs
so barely contained
they stained little fingers
winy violet.

Those dark lanterns beckoned.
and we responded,
bringing home buckets full
for pies, and cobblers,
and eating till our
lips and tongues grew dusky.

We nursed on the nipple of summer
and never questioned. Who knew
they'd last just a season or two,

and then fade away, leaving behind
the memory, and as a tease,
a solitary leaner here and there,
that would not or could not yield?

If there exists a Heaven, though,
it's full of blackberries, and eager little hands.

Round Pond

A gust writes its earthy ideology
on the pond's evanescent skin.

Every direction has its
course of dominion, she reads,
as the message blurs and changes.

O the world's complexity, it says now,
and isn't power always ebbing away?

What is probable can suddenly go doubtful,
no matter how hard your wings beat.

Winds shift and scribble all directions at once,
in sync, in sequence, at cross purposes,
so she imagines a transparent symphony
playing, whether we know it or not.

Caprice is tireless. So is interconnectedness.
Any moment, something new will be
given a little push and set in motion.

The Black Dog

Stood in the freezing rain,
thin as soot on the snow's crust,
cowering in the middle of the right lane,
with his tail between his legs,
held belly close like a guilty fist,
whole being pulled tight,
imploded
to a single
pinpoint of light
in a black void.

Both of us caught,
the same way, in the held breath,
that follows the word malignancy.

The doctor's hand on your shoulder,
his fingernails so clean and perfectly cut,
the new snow of his office coat incongruous
as the backdrop for the black dog
now frozen in front of us both
waiting to be mowed down.

*****

When the black dog enters your life,
the hairs standing up
on the back of your neck
bring it all into focus.

Dog chose you,
lying down at your feet
offered a dark companionship,
freedom, perhaps, for the first time,

from the old fears
that had chased you down
the alleyway of the years.

Dog stands guard.
There is ownership between you.
The long yellow teeth, fur glossy
and catching light, scary but familiar
enough to lull you away
from sunlight, the body,
love's itch.

For dog you have always been just right,
and this makes you lie awake
some nights, reaching down now and then
to check that its collar is still there,
cold on your fingers, studded as if with stars.

Dog lets you tune out everything else
if you want to, let's you curl up asleep,
through each day until the train, you are
riding on, gets ready to stop.

Trust Dog to nuzzle you when it's time,
lead you, like a blind man, back home.

Sloan-Kettering

I wanted to tell you
about the gypsies
in the hospital lobby,
and the four elegant ladies
in the elevator, their hair
slicked back into chignons,
their earrings gold and gleaming.

I wanted to tell you
about the hairless woman
playing piano in the solarium,
all of them waiting, waiting
on a piece of white paper,
for someone to come
out of surgery cancer-free.

All of them frozen in time,
like I was, after they wheeled
you away from me, pulled you
through the white doors,
along with all of my energy.

I wanted images and metaphors
to take me away from the dread
I felt, surrendering you to scalpels
and anesthesia, but all I could do
was take inventory in silence,
to prove I wasn't alone,
while poems hid deep inside
the whiteness of waiting,
waiting for a reprieve.

Window

It was a perfect cool glass square in a bare wall.

It was what I looked through,
my transparent body afloat
in the middle, the white hospital bed,
sitting behind me, where you slept,
post-operative and restless
in your weedy tether of tubing.

It was dark, and the Queensboro Bridge
stretched out this way and that, streaked
by headlights, blinking through us both
as time will, turning us into shadows
while the world goes on with its business.

This is the same window where a Resident
stood, framed by Botticellian blue, reeling off
a worst-case scenario: lymph nodes, cobalt,
chemo, jawbone, teeth, while we gritted ours,
like you do, on a carnival ride, as it goes belly up,
the Roosevelt Island Tram sliding away
behind him, clean as a razor.

I've never been to Roosevelt Island, but as I
waited I imagined it limned in light,
like the tram, a small bead of safety.
And I wanted to be one of the tiny people
allowed to spend some time there,
even though I could take nothing with me.
No bags, no personal items,
no one I love, not even my children.

After they returned you to me, with
better news than either of us expected,
I turned from the glass, as you woke
in wild-eyed agony, barely able
to scratch a few words on a legal pad,
asking, *Did they get it all out?*

Yes. I replied, yes, the news is good,
helped you to train your gaze,
once again on the future,
and that beautiful view,
its sparkling pool of hope.

Corn Hill at Low Tide

We wade through nature's gallery,
heads bent, backs arching like lovers
over what the water's left behind:
a sculpture garden of rock and barnacle,
bladderwrack, whelk, periwinkle, scallop shell.

How they mount one another,
make a kind of aggregate love
here in the salty shallows.

I offer you a bauble big as a Faberge egg,
with a miniature green tree
rooted to its back.
Here, take its rubbery fingers
and place them near your heart.

Reach for Me

Fold into me
like a satin bridal gown
tissue-wrapped and softly lowered
into a cedar-lined hope chest,
but never forgotten.

Slip into the folds of me
fragrantly, flatten me
like a saved bouquet
whispering delicate petals
all over a box of snapshots.

Sweet old love:
yellowed at the edges,
wistful, a reawakening,
riding a shaft of sunlight.

Reach for me,
rummage through me,
gather me to you
like generations of hands
begging remembrance.

All the hungry pink starfish.

Ode to the Moon Snail

Unlikely predator!
In that gleaming whorled shell,
its spiraled white setting tide pools alight,
agleam, O dance, O trance of hungry chalky nebula!

And languorous taster,
tongue so full and flexible
extended in its sensual narrowing gyre.
O unsuspecting quahog!

How does such glistening undulant meat
suddenly harden into drill-bit?
What salty tide is this that turns sweet seduction fierce
enough to mount and pierce such horny shell?

O Sweet clam liquefaction,
to be ravished by the moon itself!
Delicious clammy darkness
suddenly inhabited by two!

Duck Harbor

We wake early to see the sun rise,
drink coffee and eat egg sandwiches,
as a bay-wide madrigal rises with it,

sung by the muttering mallards, shrill
plovers, raspy fish crows, high twittering
sandpipers, sharp scritch of gulls
as they dive and swoop, sound rising
from every stand of marsh grass, dock
post, fish-rich ripple, salty low tide
mud swirl, even the frogs, singing
the light in, the morning wind,
the blessed stillnesses that hold us,
like infants, born of the womb of night.

A great blue heron sweeps the air overhead,
momentarily erasing all sound,
replacing it with a haunting wide-winged rest,
then the madrigal resumes its praise, this time,
the wild rain rolling in, blue and silver, as the bay
itself, all gifts accepted with equal gladness.

Mother of Pearl

The way a life builds, she thinks,
layer upon layer, each one adding
strength, making the soul
more luminous, and loved
ones more beautiful.

The way the years
and their experiences
can break or fortify
a marriage, eat away
at love's body, or
smooth out memory's
rough edges to protect
its soft tissue core.

The way pain and grief
change color, as the
angle of vision shifts,
the way damaging debris
disappears beneath resilience,
and forgiveness turns
trouble iridescent.

Not so much a miracle, she thinks,
that the shell around them is still intact
as a mystery, tied to these trips to this
outermost place, to get our bearings,
dissolve, release, solidify, forget.

Atwood Higgins House

The whole cape used to be covered in hardwoods:
oak and hickory, thick-trunked and moving
like a choir of seraphim on these hills.

Until the settlers sent them crashing down,
to be of use, as squatty clapboard houses,
and fishing boats, the tallest ones skinned,
and forced to hold up sails for the plague of ships
coming and going through these waters,
packed with people and goods.

Now dunes blow away in a season,
and most of what's left is scrub oak,
twisting low to the ground, skulking
really, intent on sticking around
by under-achieving.

As we stand here imagining
that low creaking, a symphony
of ghost songs on the wind,
I want to say, some of the cutting
we did, lets more of the light in.

But do we know, any more,
how to recognize bliss?
The way these last days of childhood
have turned into madrigal?

Beehive Oven

A small iron door opened above the hearth
its dark narrow womb-shaped place
heated with red coals from the fire.

A woman tested it by putting her arm in its mouth,
and counting till she could no longer stand the bite.
The number she reached told her the temperature, and she
adjusted things until it was right and ready for baking.

O to be bread's oracle every day, and intimate
with fire, in ways we can't be now, in this,
our body-starved age of dials and recipes.

The Body's Errand

I think, is to nuzzle the world,
to lend its dusky pile of cells
to everything it touches,
in order to be touched back,
the way snowflakes
surrender to a wind that blows
and sculpts them into drifts.

The body, I think, loves life every day,
whether the brain knows it or not.
It is the soul's embrace, it puts
a face on decency and kindness.
Its slow decay and losses bring us grace.

The body lifted by the soul's light,
and casting about, ready to do its part.

Masher

Cooking was an art to my mother.
She mashed potatoes with a delicate
metal instrument, its curving wire
lifting and whipping the smooth
white pulp into creamy mounds.

The bounce of her arm as it rose
and fell in a springy staccato,
her grip on the long wooden handle,
stopped time, turned it creamy and simple.
We happily shoveled it in in buttery mouthfuls.

My masher is more like a wooden club
left behind by some passing carnival juggler.
Potatoes huddle in the bowl, little white
skulls about to be battered and crushed,
resistant and full of lumps though they be.

I hear in its rhythm, the thump of time's
big feet, as we wolf down our meals,
and head back out to the car.

When Fog Is Afoot

it's not just the way objects rise, sinister
and ghostly, out of it, that stops us cold.
It's not the way they seem to come out of nowhere.
It's the nowhere itself, engulfing them, surrounding
us, as the air gradually fills with a lack of context:
a muffling, a mystery that scrubs away all substance,
world as *tabula rasa,* and you feel like you've
been borne to a place you don't recognize.

Cold engulfs you, your shoulders develop
a tremor, ghosts seem to lurk in the whiteness,
you think about being erased one day,
your heart running out of beats,
the body you love replaced by a story.

So, this is what growing old feels like.
What used to sustain us graying,
and going dull, until it becomes merely
a haze in your head, out of which familiar
images rise, until one day you realize,
you barely recognize what's left.

Then it's about accepting
this temporary blindness,
which, like vapor, will burn
off in the growing light.

Wellfleet Pier

Bikes. Two boys in cut-offs
hurling themselves like stones into the bay,
as tourists lean over the pilings,
eyeing the cold steel swirling surface
as boy upon boy churns it into froth,
then sinks, hands crossed over his chest,
quick as blinking, nothing but ink
and eddies curling above him.

You can see the relief on their faces
as what seems like a bloodless hand bobs up first,
attached to an arm that bursts out
and grabs at the ladder.

This is the story they tell
as boy upon boy upon boy upon boy
first plunges into uncertainty,
then corpse-like, lands and dies awhile,
until he is reborn and cutting the water knife-like,
swims back toward the light and safety of shore.

This is the story we came so far to hear.
One of the men says he used to do this too,
for hours on end, and we nod,
trying to hold on to this catch of the day,
slipperier than a fish.

Whale Watch

As if deep water solidified,
and rose out of a wave crest, slapping
hard at the surface, a thing they call
breaching, a fissure, a rupture, a rift,
through which they are born of the salty mother,
enormous angels breaking into the light,
black and shiny as coal before it ignites,
great beasts made of sugar-crusted licorice.

Slim winged Humpbacks, bedecked in barnacles,
slapping the water, great cows vocalizing
as they feed, their throat-groove purses
expanding with krill, and small schooling fish.
Working together, swimming in circles,
to trap clouds of silver protein in bubble nets
they rise through, mouths open, straining it all
through baleen plates, as we sit atop
their dinner table, watching,

Occasionally, one of them spy-hops to get a look at us,
snout sticking out eye high, these creatures, big as buses,
their four chambered hearts weighing as much as three men.
Large-hearted Leviathans singing love songs in eight octaves,
songs complex as symphonies, songs big enough to fill
a cathedral. We try to read their tail flukes as they dive
into that long, compacted, mysterious night below.
You know, a young woman says, *people used to believe
the earth was borne on the back of a whale.
They've existed for fifteen million years.
We humans certainly pale in comparison to that*!

The biologist on board chimes in, tells us a Humpback
got herself hopelessly ensnared, a while ago,
in some crab lines off the Farallon Islands,

near San Francisco. And when divers
cut her loose she inscribed her elation
by swimming around them in circles, and then
nudging each one of her rescuers, before swimming off.
That's a whale of a handshake, a thank you they'll never forget.
They've been known to defend gray whale calves
from Pilot Whales or Orcas, trumpeting at them
and lob-tailing long after the whole thing has come
to its awful end, as if to express horror, indignation, empathy.
Orcas kill their calves too. *Orcas have to eat,* an old man says.
They're predators. They can't help it.
It's humans the whales need to worry about.

The planet is changing, the oceans are warming.
We keep on polluting and factory-fishing.
Shellfish go toxic and poison mackerel,
then mackerel poison the whales.
And they're beaching themselves to get away from
our Sonar. It makes them crazy: their brains bleed,
their ears bleed, they get lesions on their organs,
some of them die of the bends.

Just as he finishes saying this, one slides up to the hull,
calm and curious. She rolls sideways, her round eye black
as a gap in the stars, gazing up at our faces,
so pale and diminutive, as we lean over
the railing of this drifting white hulk stalking her daily.
Her rough skin gleams. *Beautiful,* our children murmur,
and she meets the hush, that comes over us, with a look
both knowing and patient, a mother's look, a warrior's look,
all amplitude and sorrow, before she rolls away.

Another Word for Mother Is Water

When one of them, or the other, grows a shell,
you have to squint across golden light,
and offer encouragement. *Better,* you say,
*for staying afloat, for gliding, for going the distance,
for snapping up whatever comes your way.* You have to
liquify and flow into these moments, awash
though you are, in worried confusion.

Love is a funny thing, isn't it?

Another word for the nuzzle of cheek against cheek,
an image you can't seem to shake, though Lord knows,
it makes you ache to hold on to it, hold them back.
So little time left to drink in their slow grace
as they comb their hair on the beach,
or sit on a flowered towel watching the waves.

This is how it goes: two turtles, swimming,
me swimming beside them, in what has now
become their element: that cool green silence
above waving water grass, until I can't touch bottom:
my signal to return to the beach, where my heart,
in its cage of bone, can search for other words
for love, that involve *letting go, having confidence,
trusting the element they move through,
to hold them up while they're out of reach.*

Special

He looks to be fifteen or so, as he sits in the shallows,
and plays with a water bottle for almost an hour,
watching it float, pressing it under the water,
until it bubbles and fills, then pouring it out
from different heights, plunging it straight down,
to hear it gulp and gurgle, watching the way it drinks
as he bends his body over it, serious as a scientist.

Every move he makes, every piece of water
choreography is a revelation: the way it pours
over his chest, the loud sound it makes as it hits
the pond's rippled surface, the burp, the slap and hizzle,
the splarge, slosh and wheeze of water's infinite song.

O to study the world one thing at a time, the way this boy,
we call imperfect, does. O to be a small god, transforming
the commonplace to the sacred with your play!

Kite

A delicate bird
floating, silent
in the steady wind,
oblivious, detached,
and out of reach,
above the tired fishermen
toting poles and empty
buckets to the car,
the line of beach-chaired women
trading stories, mouths ajar
their laughter interweaving
with the screech and
whine of hungry gulls,
the whoops from teenage boys
riding the waves in wetsuits,
looking like happy seals
until they rise out of the surf
and drag their boogie boards
behind them on the sand,
the wild applause as newlyweds
make their entrance at the Surf Club,
and the band kicks in so they can
begin their Mr. and Mrs. dance.

All the while, kite leans,
shimmies, then steadies above it all,
like the lives we put on hold to come here,
attached to us by invisible string.
Here is our chance to see
how beautiful they look at a distance,
how normal, even happy, as time,
like the wind, pushes hard.
How gracefully they hold.

About the Author

Eileen Moeller lives in southern New Jersey with her husband Charles, a psychologist. Born in 1950, and raised in Paterson NJ, she lived for twenty-five years in Central New York state, where she earned an M.A. in Creative Writing from Syracuse University. She has had a lifetime of poems appear intermittently in high school and college literary magazines, newsletters, newspapers, literary journals, and anthologies. She has four books: *Firefly, Brightly Burning* (Grayson Books, 2015), *The Girls in Their Iron Shoes* (Finishing Line Press, 2017), *Silk City Sparrow* (Read Furiously Inc., 2020), and *Waterlings* (Word Tech Communications Inc., 2023).

Read her blog, And So I Sing: Poems and Iconography, at eileenmoeller.blogspot.com

www.ingramcontent.com/pod-product-compliance
Lightning Source LLC
Chambersburg PA
CBHW071332190426
43193CB00041B/1751